D1368427

WRITING NOTES

WITH A

PERSONAL

TOUCH

WRITING NOTES

WITH A

PERSONAL TOUCH

Daria Price Bowman
and Maureen LaMarca

Photographs by Michael Grand

Doubleday Book & Music Clubs, Inc.
Garden City, New York

A GUILDAMERICA BOOKS®/FRIEDMAN GROUP BOOK

Michael Friedman Publishing Group, Inc.
15 West 26 Street
New York, New York 10010

GuildAmerica Books® is a trademark of Doubleday Book & Music Clubs, Inc.

Photographs © 1994 Michael Grand

ISBN 1-56865-078-7

WRITING NOTES WITH A PERSONAL TOUCH was prepared and produced by Michael Friedman Publishing Group, Inc.
15 West 26th Street
New York, New York 10010

Editor: Karla Olson
Designer: Susan Livingston
Art Director: Jeff Batzli
Photography Director: Christopher C. Bain
Calligraphy: Anthony Bloch

Color separations by
Bright Arts (Hong Kong) Ltd.
Printed and bound in China by
Leefung-Asco Printers, Ltd.

Dedicated with love to Ernie, Sam, and Cassie. With special thanks to my mother and father, Carl and Elizabeth Price, for sharing with me their love of language.

DPB

For Sal, Susan, and Rebecca with love.

MBL

Michael Friedman Publishing Group gratefully acknowledges the assistance of Crane and Company, Inc., Dalton, MA; Kate's Paperie, New York, NY; and Dempsey & Carroll, Stationers and Engravers, New York, NY.

Grateful acknowledgment is also made for props used in the photographs to The Amber Palette, New York, NY; Lynn's Card and Gift, New York, NY; Kate's Paperie, New York, NY; Arthur Brown, New York, NY; LS Collection, New York, NY; State Office Supply Company, New York, NY.

Table of Contents

Dear Barbara,

I just put in my rose border. It took the better part of the weekend, but I'm delighted with it. Sam is building a bench for the garden and we plan to place it where the scent is most wonderful so you and I can sit and sip iced tea and enjoy.

Let's plan a little get-together the first or second weekend in August.

Love,
Linda

1

Ways to Say You Care

I long for a letter from you!

–Princess Alice of England,
lonely for her mother, Queen Victoria.

Ah! A letter!

It stands out, a rose-tinted envelope hand-addressed with navy blue ink, a gem amid a pile of bills, junk mail, catalogs, and magazines. There's practically a radiance to it.

We love to get letters. It brings a wonderful feeling of warmth to know that someone took the time to send a greeting, to share a bit of news, to reassure us about a difficulty, to exclaim over an outrageous incident, to comfort when in pain, or to send a sentimental photo.

Whether two short sentences or several pages of long and chatty paragraphs, a letter has magic. But we must all remember that sending one is still the best way to receive one.*

If you've gotten away from letter writing, or if you think it is too time consuming to fit into your busy schedule, consider this: Letter writing can actually be a more efficient way to keep in touch than the telephone. A simple "Hi, how are you" to Aunt Nancy can be penned in five minutes, while a call could ramble on indefinitely. And it could be a very pricey chat depending on where Aunt Nancy lives, while a letter costs only the price of a stamp.

Your letter and mother's have come at last! I was so glad to get them I cried.

Anne Sullivan Macy to Helen Keller, her beloved pupil and lifelong friend.

Letter writing has other lovely benefits, too. It can be a calming, centering experience. It can help you de-stress and set aside the day's frustrations while you bring friends closer, enrich social relationships, and inspire love. It's so much nicer to read and savor news from an old friend at your leisure, rather than taking her call while you're rushing to get dinner or dashing off to a meeting. Worst of all, you may procrastinate for weeks, even months before you call a dear friend because you're busy or you fear catching her at an awkward or harried moment. A letter, however, can be read and savored when the time is right, and just a few words will refresh her spirits and yours.

A letter can be a quick impression of a film or play you'd like a friend to see, or a short, one-paragraph description for Grandma of something Janie accomplished. Indeed, it's a very effective way to make someone feel involved in your life though he or she may be absent.

If there is a "secret" to good letter writing, it is simply to write as you speak. It's easy when you write as if you're

Mom,

We wish you could have been with us for Janie's first piano recital. She was terrific! All your extra help last summer surely helped her play even more beautifully.

Love,
Cheryl

speaking directly to your correspondent, using words and phrases you always use. Stamp your letter with your personality. If you attempt to make use of formal or stilted language, you'll waste a great deal of time and energy for no reason at all.

For example, forget the stilted:

I encountered two mutual friends at the Annual Meeting of the Association of Rose Growers on the 25th.

Instead, say:

Mary, I met two old friends of ours—Joanne and Mildred—at the yearly rose growers' meeting last week.

Make your concern the message, not the words. Let your words flow so that the person receiving your note can almost see and hear you while reading. Don't worry about rules of grammar, margins, or crossing out, and never "compose" a letter to a loved one, friend, or child. If you think writing a letter is all about impressing your friends or loved ones with pages of literary prose, you'll never write one.

> *All* letters, methinks, should be as free and easy as one's discourse, not studied as an oration, nor made up of hard words like a charm.
>
> Dorothy Osborne, Lady Temple
> (1627–1695)

An alternative to writing a letter—picking out a greeting card—may serve your purpose in a pinch, but can a jingle writer's sentiments really express your own heartfelt get-well wish, congratulations for a birthday or an accomplishment, or the emotion you feel for someone you've fallen in love with?

Here, for example, is an excerpt from a famous love letter of a time when greeting cards weren't fashionable. The thought is so original and written with a great deal of feeling. Think of the effect your own letter, written this way, could have on its recipient.

> *I am very uneasy, my love, at receiving no news of you; write me quickly four pages—pages full of agreeable things which shall fill my heart with the pleasantest feelings. I hope before long to crush you in my arms and cover you with a million kisses.*
>
> **—Napoleon Bonaparte to Josephine Beauharnais**

If "starting" is a problem for you (even accomplished authors get rattled by a blank sheet of paper), try asking yourself what your recipient would enjoy hearing. Or focus on the incident or thought that made you decide to write to this person in the first place—you ran across a photo of a time you spent to-

gether or you finished a book she recommended. Start with this, and the rest of the letter is likely to come easily.

Probably the very worst way to start a letter is: "I meant to write sooner, but I just couldn't find the time." It's like saying, "I would have written sooner, but I had more important things to do. You weren't my priority."

Perhaps you can draw some inspiration from these first sentences written to intimate relatives or friends by well-known historical figures:

> **It was a perfect delight to see your well-known handwriting again!**
>
> **—Mark Twain**

> **Truth is such a rare thing, it is so delightful to tell it.**
>
> **—Emily Dickinson**

> **I send you a little line, and shake your hand across the water.**
>
> **—William Makepeace Thackeray**

Setting the proper mood is extremely important to writing a heartfelt letter. Make sure you position yourself where you are comfortable so your thoughts and feelings will flow. Pour a glass of wine or light a scented candle as you begin. Relax outside on the patio after a long day as the sun is setting, or put your feet up near a crackling fire.

Treat yourself to some beautiful papers. Check specialty shops or department stores for different looks that express your individuality—creamy whites, ivories, pinks, pale blues or lavenders, hot fuchsias, cards with bright borders, or art postcards. Try different sizes and textures and splurge on a lovely fountain pen or some colored pencils. Have fun with inks in shades such as Caribbean blue, midnight black, or apple red. Store papers, pens, and your address book in a nice basket to eliminate the hunt for supplies or zip codes when you're ready to write.

Remember! You don't need a whole afternoon, an entire evening, or a vacation setting to write a letter. George Washington, Ralph Waldo Emerson, Virginia Woolf, Jane Austen, Abraham Lincoln, Mark Twain, and Winston Churchill were all conscientious letter writers who took time from busy, full lives to correspond regularly with friends. Lincoln, it is said, was often too busy to eat or sleep, but never too busy to write the letters he wanted to write. Benjamin Franklin simply enjoyed the process. Each left marvelous pieces of their lives behind in their letters.

For THERE IS A TIME...FOR EVERY PURPOSE AND FOR EVERY WORK.

—

Ecclesiastes

A letter, even the simplest of notes, is a document. And every document should include the date it was written. While most of our letters will not wind up in museums or important collections, some may be kept for years, even generations, for sentimental reasons or as part of personal family treasures. Always put a date, including the day, month, and year, on your notes. Place it at the top on either the right or left side. A very old-fashioned (and attractive) approach is to place the date in the lower left-hand corner of a one-page letter or note. This is especially appropriate for a response to an invitation.

Start developing the habit today. Letter writing may involve some reprogramming, but the harvest of friendship and goodwill will be well worth the effort.

2

Love

and Friendship

The only way to have a friend

is to be one.

—Ralph Waldo Emerson

Every day, we make phone calls to friends, associates, and loved ones to express our thoughts and ideas. But a phone call is a fleeting thing. It provides no lasting record. Love letters and notes of friendship, on the other hand, are tangible. And they are the easiest letters to write because they come straight from the heart. In this chapter, we look at ways you can put your feelings on paper and feel comfortable doing it.

Today, few of us are in the habit of writing love letters. We are inhibited and often re-luctant to commit our emotions to paper. Besides, it's just so easy to pick up the tele-phone. Somehow the thought of love notes slipped into rose-scented envelopes tied up with pink ribbons doesn't seem to fit with high-tech life in the nineties.

Or does it? A love letter doesn't have to be a literary masterpiece; it needs only to capture sincere feelings.

The first few days of a love affair can be that much sweeter if the lovers dare to express their thoughts on paper. Imagine how special someone would feel to receive a letter like the one from Alyssa to Roger (right).

Be sure to write Personal on the envelope—and don't send it to his office!

Writing love letters should not be re-stricted to starry-eyed lovers. Dear friends

> *BREVITY MAY BE THE SOUL OF WIT, BUT NOT WHEN SOMEONE'S SAYING "I LOVE YOU."*
> —
> *Judith Viorst*

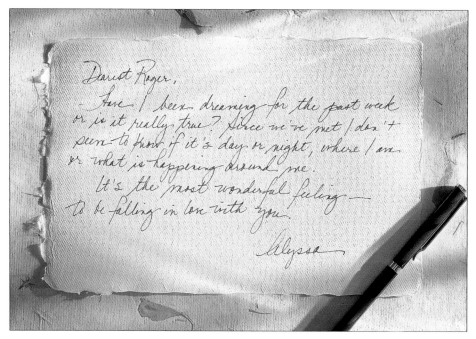

Darest Roger,

Have I been dreaming for the past week or is it really true? Since we've met I don't seem to know if it's day or night, where I am or what is happening around me.

It's the most wonderful feeling — to be falling in love with you.

Alyssa

who care deeply for each other can also communicate their feelings with intimate, warm notes that bring joy and pleasure to the recipient. A quickly scrawled note such as the one at the beginning of the book will bring a smile to your old friend's face.

Send a simple note to a sibling, aunt, uncle, or other family member when he or she is about to be married, move, change jobs, retire, have a baby, divorce, start a company, take a vacation, or for any other occasion. They will enjoy knowing you are thinking of them.

Eric—

I heard that you're taking the family white-water rafting. I'm absolutely *green* with envy. Looking forward to hearing all about it when you return.

Best, Sean

Pick up a few postcards when you are out of town on business or on vacation. Then, whenever you think of a friend, a relative, or a special someone, send one of the cards with a little note that tells the thought. To make it even easier, keep a supply of postcard stamps handy so the spontaneity of your thoughts won't be hampered by the need to run to the post office.

Keep a calendar of your friends' and loved ones' birthdays so that you can send cards. And always include a few personal words, instead of relying on the printed message on the card. After all, how can someone who is paid to write hundreds of messages and rhymes know what is in your heart?

At holiday time, be sure to write a few lines on your cards. Save the cards with your name printed on them for business associates; friends and relatives should receive a more personal greeting.

Send your mother and father a loving note on your birthday. It's an especially nice way to tell them how much you appreciate their love and encouragement. After all, the day you were born was a very special one in their lives, too.

When you have a roll of snapshots developed, have duplicates made so you can send them to family and friends. It's a wonderful opportunity to stay in touch and it requires so little effort.

Simply enclose a photo or two in a blank note card and write a few lines about them.

Write a note to your best friend for no reason at all. Tell her that you're feeling a bit sad, happy, nervous, excited, bored—whatever you are feeling at that particular time. If you do express feelings of sadness and you are not a regular letter writer, be sure to communicate that it's just a passing thing or she will surely worry about you.

Writing notes of friendship and love is really just an extension of your loving thoughts. By letting yourself be true to your emotions, and with a little practice, you'll soon be sharing your love with those special people in your life.

*W*OMEN'S PROPENSITY TO SHARE CONFIDENCES IS UNIVERSAL. WE CONFIRM OUR REALITY BY SHARING.

—

Barbara Grizzuti Harrison

*P*AINS OF LOVE BE SWEETER FAR THAN ALL OTHER PLEASURES ARE.

—

John Dryden (1631–1701)

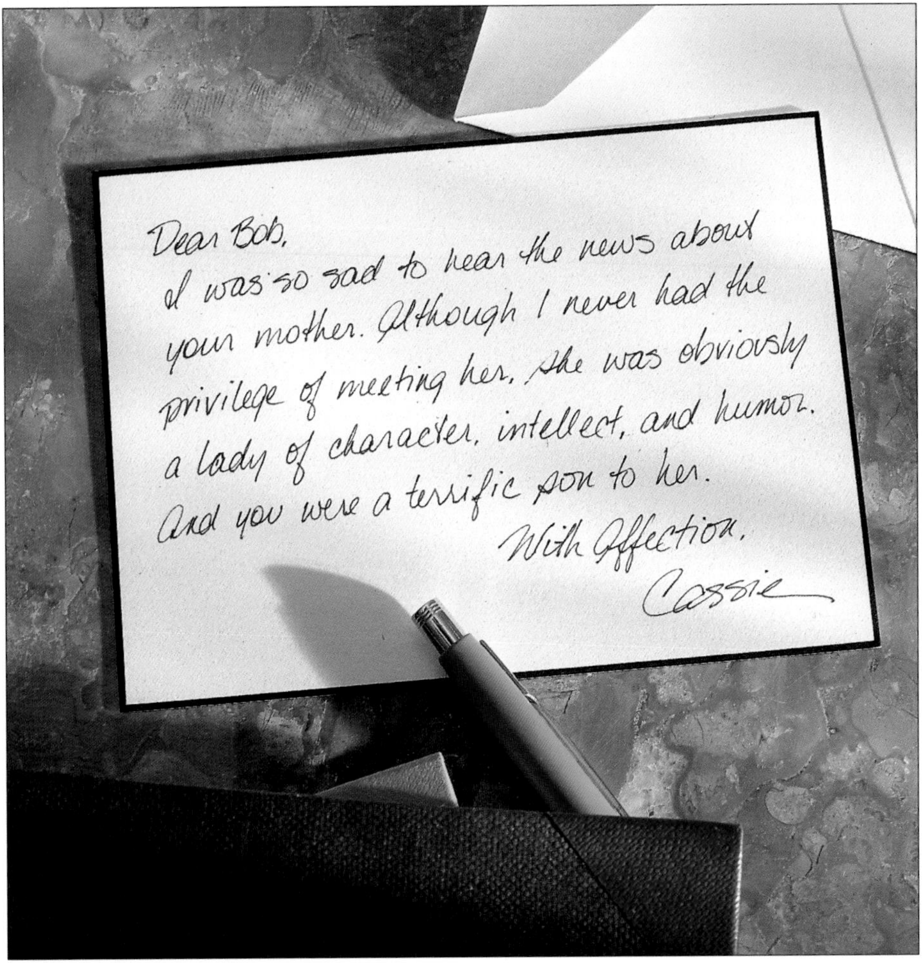
Dear Bob,
I was so sad to hear the news about
your mother. Although I never had the
privilege of meeting her, she was obviously
a lady of character, intellect, and humor.
And you were a terrific son to her.
With Affection,
Cassie

Sympathy

*A fated sorrow may be lighted
with words.*

–from the Latin

Condolences or sympathy notes are what we write in the event of a death, a serious illness, and other instances that cause grief and emotional trauma. This chapter will help you navigate this sad and uncomfortable, but important, responsibility.

No letter is harder to write than one regarding a sad event. Condolences or sympathy notes are intensely personal and emotional. For some people they are truly too painful to attempt because one's own sorrows are brought achingly close to the surface. However, writing a thoughtful letter to a friend who is experiencing a period of sadness or pain is a kind and gracious act that will be dearly appreciated.

Keep in mind that the death of a loved one is not the only time this kind of letter should be written. When a close friend is having troubles of any kind, a short note to let her know you are thinking of her will be a welcome respite. The loss of a job is a devastating blow for any-

*I*F I CAN STOP ONE HEART FROM BREAKING,

I SHALL NOT LIVE IN VAIN;

IF I CAN EASE ONE LIFE THE ACHING,

OR COOL ONE PAIN,

OR HELP ONE FAINTING ROBIN

UNTO HIS NEST AGAIN,

I SHALL NOT LIVE IN VAIN.

Emily Dickinson, Life

one. The failure of a project, the rejection of a manuscript, the loss of a treasured piece of jewelry, the illness of a close family member, a fire or flood in a home—all such disasters, large or small, exact a terrible toll from those who experience them. By penning a short note to show that you sympathize with your friend's loss, you will help to lighten the burden of pain or sorrow.

Try to write naturally, the way you might speak on the phone. Start out with your first reaction.

I couldn't believe it when I heard that your family's cabin burned. What an awful loss for all of you.

$\mathcal{L}$OYAL WORDS
HAVE THE
SECRET OF
HEALING
GRIEF.
–
*Menander
(342–290 B.C.)*

Never point out silver linings. Instead, commiserate. Sometimes it's appropriate to reminisce.

I will always treasure memories of my visits with your family at the cabin.

When someone you love loses a good friend, you validate that friendship by acknowledging the loss. Be generous with your praise for the devotion and love that was shared.

If you read the obituary of someone you knew and admired, think about sending a condolence to the husband, wife, or another survivor. It is very comforting to the grieving family to know that their loved one was held in your esteem. Even a simple note represents a generous and kind act on your part. It is such a small effort but it will be deeply appreciated.

Years ago, I worked with Bill. He was a good, honest businessman and I liked him very much. You have my heartfelt sympathy.

Death after a prolonged illness is often a relief for the survivors. Writing a note of sympathy in this situation is frequently a difficult task. Be careful not to express such sentiments as "it's a blessing;" instead, write words of comfort.

*S*ORROW'S
CROWN OF
SORROW IS
REMEMBERING
THINGS.
—
Alfred, Lord
Tennyson
(1850–1892)

I know how difficult these past months have been for you and your family. You have been – and will continue to be – in my thoughts and prayers.

Think about sending a short note when a friend or relative loses an old pet. For most people, a dog or cat is a member of the family, and the death of that animal leaves a wound. Don't ever suggest a replacement pet! Instead try to paint a written picture of your memory of the pet and its owner.

Avoid printed sympathy cards. Although they do make the task easier, *they are so totally impersonal. Instead, select simple white, gray, cream, or blue note paper. A heavy, plain stock, perhaps with a simple band border or your monogram, is appropriate.*

While none of us enjoys the task of expressing sorrow, it may be helpful to keep in mind that the person who receives even the shortest of personal messages may find solace and serenity at a dark and lonely moment. Remembering a phone call does not have the same consoling power as rereading the words of a friend. Your few well-chosen words could mean the difference between continued pain and the road to healing.

Dear Jane,
I'm so very sorry to hear about Whiskers' death. Twenty years is such a long time to live with a cat - longer than you've lived with Tom and the boys! Not having her around - bad habits and all - will take a lot of getting used to. If there is a cat heaven, she is sure to be there. And you know she'll be in charge!
Fondly, Dee Dee.

𝓛OOK IN THY HEART AND WRITE.

—

Sir Philip Sidney
(1554–1586)

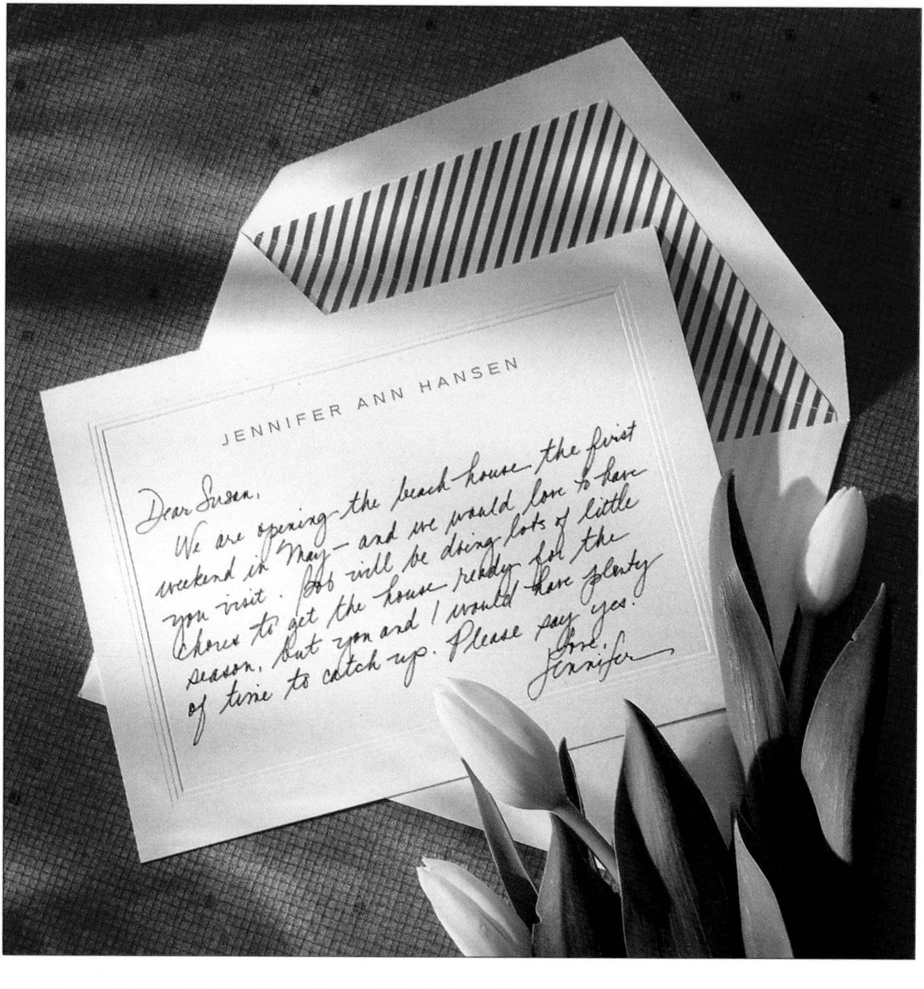
JENNIFER ANN HANSEN
Dear Susan,
We are opening the beach house the first
weekend in May — and we would love to have
you visit. Bob will be doing lots of little
chores to get the house ready for the
season, but you and I would have plenty
of time to catch up. Please say yes.
Love,
Jennifer

CHAPTER
4

Invitations

*Welcome
is the best cheer.*

—Greek proverb

*I*n days of old, ladies sat in private parlors and penned elegant invitations on thick white paper in accordance with the strict social customs of their time.

Today, there is less structured formality in social life than at any other time in history. Often we'll simply pick up the telephone to make a date for dinner or extend an impromptu invitation when we run into a friend or neighbor on our round of Saturday-morning errands.

However, there is still a certain protocol that governs the handling of invitations, which can be categorized as "formal," "semiformal," and "informal."

Formal

The engraved third-person invitation is perhaps the final holdout of the high formality that once typified proper manners and social correctness. Most of us will make use of this type of invitation for only the most special circumstances. A wedding, for instance, a ceremonious dinner, or a milestone anniversary may warrant such treatment. An elegant way to extend this invitation is to have it engraved on luxurious heavy stationery.

For the most formal event, an invitation should look like one from Judge and Mrs. Cruthers. Reputable stationers and printers are well qualified to make helpful recommendations about wording, type, and other considerations.

Equally as elegant is the fill-in formal invitation generally used by hostesses who do a fair amount of formal entertaining, like Mr. and Mrs. Golden.

Judge and Mrs. Marshall Edward Cruthers

request the honour of your presence

at the marriage of their daughter

Nancy Margaret

to

Mr. Phillip Andrew Lynden

on Friday, the twentieth of May

at six o'clock in the evening

The Cathedral of Saint Philip

Atlanta, Georgia

Mr. and Mrs. Thomas Golden

request the pleasure of

Mr. and Mrs. James Allen's

company at dinner

on Friday, May 15

at 7 o'clock

333 Cold Spring Road

Cranford, New Jersey 07016

R.s.v.p.

Mr. and Mrs. Ernest B. Howard, Jr.
request the pleasure of

Ms. Deborah Greenberg's

company on the occasion of
their 25th anniversary dinner
on Thursday the seventeenth of March
at seven o'clock
The Woods Hole Golf Club

R.s.v.p.
100 Maker Lane
Falmouth, Massachusetts

The invitation that is entirely hand-written, such as this from Mr. and Mrs. Howard, is a striking piece if one can find the time for it. You may employ a calligrapher to pen the invitations or you can try your own hand at calligraphy and enjoy the satisfaction and sense of accomplishment that comes with doing the work yourself. There are many good books available that provide instruction in this time-honored form or you may find courses offered in your community.

Calligraphy does create a special, important personality for your once-in-a-lifetime event. It's used for presidential inaugurations, in upper corporate echelons for important events, and for other very formal social occasions. It is an elegant, sophisticated touch that conveys a sense of priority and specialness.

Of course, the formal, third-person invitation can be handwritten with a fountain pen, but regardless of the writing instrument, proper form must be followed. White or cream paper is still the preferred choice for occasions of this type.

Semiformal

For semiformal occasions such as a tea, a reception to meet a guest, or a retirement dinner—not quite black tie, but a dressy, very important occasion nonetheless—it was once customary for a woman to use her visiting card to extend the invitation.

Retirement Dinner

Mr. and Mrs. Allen Jay Fannin

15 Long Court
6 o'clock
Sunday February 7

The use of these engraved visiting cards is considered somewhat old-fashioned today, but it may be a custom worth reviving. Consider that the visiting card could actually be a time-saving device, eliminating the need for selecting invitations.

A fill-in card such as this from Mr. and Mrs. Stein may also be used for a semiformal affair. Such cards are gener-

You are invited by
Mr. & Mrs. J.P. Stein

For *Luncheon*
On *October 15*
At *1 o'clock*

15 Morningside Lane
Chatham, NJ

ally printed on a neutral stock. They often have bright borders, as well as a stylized, non-traditional typeface.

Informal

For a buffet supper, bridal shower, cocktail party, or other informal occasion, fill-in invitations are popular and acceptable. These cards are designed to suit a wide variety of personal tastes, from reproductions of the work of French impressionists or other artists available in museum stores to handmade papers adorned with lace and ribbon.

An alternative is a card known as an "informal," such as Mrs. Fannin's. An informal is a small, fold-over card that's correct and practical for invitations.

High-quality, plain white informals are readily available at all stationers. If you choose, they can be engraved, thermographed, or printed with your name or monogram.

Mrs. Allen Jay Fannin

Cocktails and Buffet Supper
Sunday, August 13th
6 o'clock
14 Sisson Court

Of course, as with the semiformal occasion, personal calling cards make a practical invitation for all types of informal occasions as well.

Finally, the casual letter of invitation written to a friend is worthy of mention. Again, write as you would speak, and your friend is sure to be delighted to join you.

Replies

If you wish to request a reply in your formal, semiformal, or informal invitation, the following forms are acceptable:

R.s.v.p. This is one of the most commonly used forms. It is the abbreviation for "Répondez s'il vous plaît," French for "Please reply." To be strictly correct, only the first letter should be capitalized. When an invitation includes this notation, a reply is a must.

Other preferences include "Please reply," "The favor of a reply is requested," and "Please address reply to (address)."

If the R.s.v.p. is followed by a phone number, your guests should attempt to reach you by phone. If they are unsuccessful, they should send a brief note or a postcard. The wording of the reply should "match" the invitation. (See "Acceptances and Regrets.")

The proper position for the reply request is in the lower left-hand corner of the invitation. It should appear a bit smaller than the message.

The gift of an invitation is always a compliment, a sincere form of flattery. It means the pleasure of one's company is desired and requested. Depending on the event, it can be one of the highest forms of social or professional courtesy.

Receiving one in the mail can brighten an entire day and create a variety of good feelings—joy, anticipation, and a sense of belonging are only a few. The more invitations you extend, the more you will receive.

Here are a few final hints for writing personal invitations:

Choose stationery to fit the occasion. Today there are thousands of styles, shapes, colors, and textures to choose that can help you communicate the particular flavor of the event.

Don't just reach for a pen. An invitation is so much more special when written with a fountain pen, a colored marker, or an assortment of colored pencils. Try a turquoise ink on white or beige paper, navy on ivory, or green on yellow. It's fun to experiment.

For a child's birthday party invitation, cut a fun shape from construction paper—a yellow tulip with a green stem for a "garden party," for example.

Think about including dried flowers, confetti, or glitter with an informal invitation to a theme party or a big get-together. Keep in mind, however, that some people—particularly those who can't stand a mess—might find this annoying.

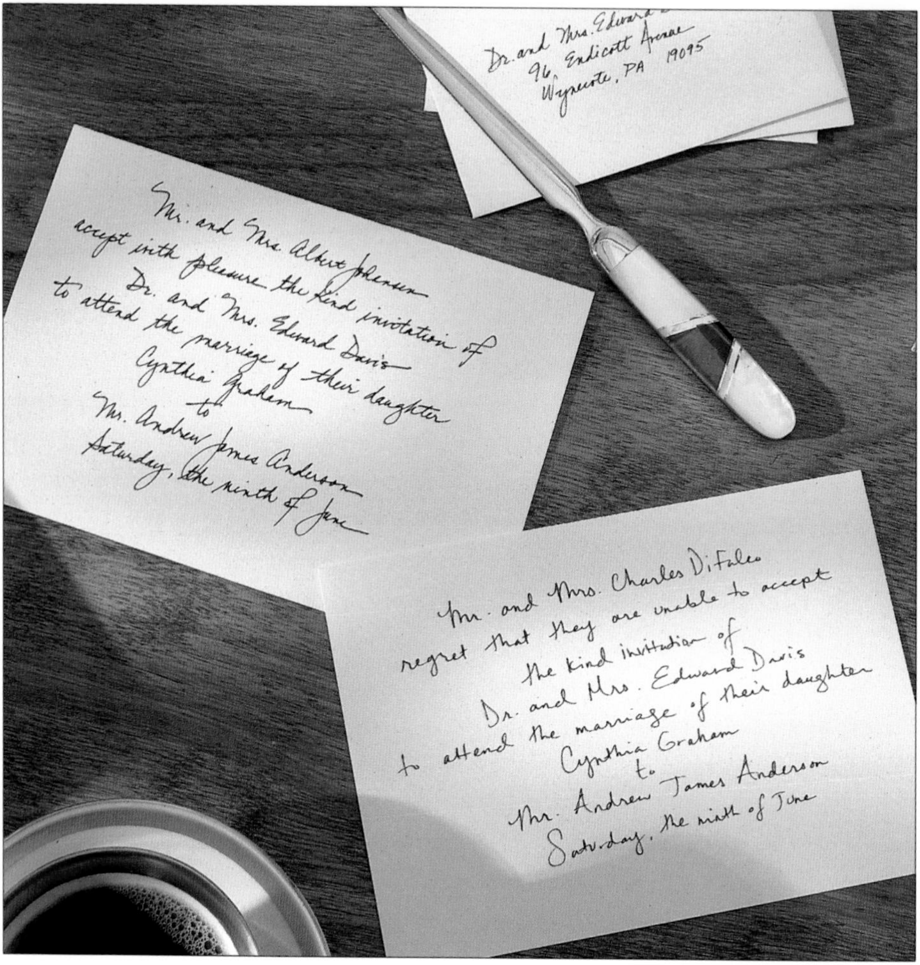
Dr. and Mrs. Edward
96 Endicott Avenue
Wyncote, PA 19095
Mr. and Mrs. Albert Johnson
accept with pleasure the kind invitation of
Dr. and Mrs. Edward Davis
to attend the marriage of their daughter
Cynthia Graham
to
Mr. Andrew James Anderson
Saturday, the ninth of June
Mr. and Mrs. Charles DiFalco
regret that they are unable to accept
the kind invitation of
Dr. and Mrs. Edward Davis
to attend the marriage of their daughter
Cynthia Graham
to
Mr. Andrew James Anderson
Saturday, the ninth of June

5

Acceptances
and Regrets

*Good manners have much to do with
emotions. To make them ring true, one
must feel them, not merely exhibit them.*

—Amy Vanderbilt

Do you know how to make a formal written reply to an engraved wedding invitation? Most people today do not. In our fast-paced existence, we tend to look for ways to speed things up, to trim time from our efforts, to make work easier. In this section, you will see how simple it is to add a little elegance and finesse to your social activities.

In days gone by, wedding invitations and other formal, printed invitations were unaccompanied by reply cards with matching return envelopes. Today, these little conveniences have become the standard—made that much easier because, more often than not, the envelopes are already stamped!

Less formal invitations usually feature an "R.s.v.p." or a crisp "Regrets Only" line with a phone number in the lower left hand corner. Often, when you call to respond, you are asked to leave a message on an answering machine. The whole process has become very impersonal.

While formal letters of acceptance and regret may be deemed somewhat archaic, think about the recipient. How much more exciting it is to receive a stack of letters telling you who will be at your wedding! And how much less disappointing to receive a formal letter or personal note than a little self-addressed, self-stamped card with the "will not attend" box checked off!

Sincere
WORDS ARE
NOT GRAND.
—
*Chinese
proverb*

If you receive a formal invitation to a wedding, debutante ball, tea, charity function, or other event and no reply card is enclosed, you must reply in writing. Keep in mind, however, that etiquette expert Emily Post says you should always use the reply card if it is included with the invitation. If you don't you will only confuse matters for your hostess.

Here is how to write a formal letter of acceptance. Follow the language of the invitation, as in the Johansens' acceptance on page 36.

If you cannot attend, then write your regrets as the DiFalcos did.

If the old-fashioned, formal acceptance format is not your style, try a slightly less formal approach, like the Frenchs', below, left.

Less formal regrets might be worded like the Frenchs', below, right.

We are delighted that we are able to attend the marriage of your daughter Cynthia Graham on Saturday, the ninth of June.

Carol and Howard French

We are disappointed that we are unable to attend the marriage of your daughter Cynthia Graham on Saturday, the ninth of June.

Carol and Howard French

You may be more comfortable with an informal note of regret like Beth and Mark's (below).

Dear Al and Katie,

Mark and I are thrilled at the prospect of attending Cindy and Andy's wedding. After all, we've known Cindy all her life. We can't wait for the big day.

Fondly, Beth

Dear Al and Katie,

Thank you for inviting us to Cindy's wedding. We are so terribly disappointed that we won't be able to attend.

Chris is graduating from college that weekend and we will be with him for several days.

We will be thinking of you all on that exciting day.

Fondly,
Beth and Mark

If you are planning to attend the wedding, you can also write an informal acceptance letter, such as this from Beth (above).

Send a handwritten note of acceptance or regret rather than phoning your response to an informal invitation for a party, luncheon, dinner, or other event. Use a blank card, a small folded note, or your visiting card (if you use them). Your message can be short and simple.

Wish we could be there on the tenth, but we'll be out of town. Thanks for thinking of us.

or

We haven't been to a card party in years. We're looking forward to the sixteenth.

If you cannot accept an invitation, it is always courteous to give the reason why on your informal response. In the past, an acknowledgment was all that was required, with no explanation necessary. Today, however, such a practice is considered somewhat ungracious. There is no need to go into great detail about your reasons for not attending. Just be straightforward and honest.

We already have plans that evening.

or

We will have guests visiting from out of town.

Adding a touch of formality to your life need not be inconvenient or time-consuming. A quickly penned response will take less time than a phone call if you are in the habit of keeping notepaper, a nice pen, stamps, and your address book handy. Your feeling of accomplishment and the recipient's appreciation will make any extra effort worthwhile.

Sept. 19
Dear Bette Ann,
How marvelous that you've completed requirements for your Ph.D! (I ran into your sister at the nature study center this afternoon.) I don't know how you ever found the time to fit all that work into your busy schedule. This will create wonderful opportunities for you that you so well deserve.
A job well done!
Fondly,
Rebecca

Congratulations

*O Wonderful, wonderful,
and most wonderful wonderful!*

–Shakespeare, from *As You Like It*

Unlike letters expressing condolence or gratitude, a letter of congratulation is not a social requirement, but it is perhaps for this reason that such a letter is so treasured.

A congratulatory note is one of the simplest letters you can write, and one that shouldn't be reserved for birthdays or marriages alone. Congratulations are in order whenever something wonderful has happened—an honor or a distinction has come to someone you know, someone has graduated or met a long-term goal, a child has been born or adopted, a graduation has taken place, or a friend has just made a business deal.

...AS MUCH GOODWILL MAY BE CONVEYED IN ONE HEARTY WORD AS IN MANY.

—

Charlotte Bronte, Jane Eyre

Pour out your joy, your excitement, and your praise. Delight with your friend. Forget about proper form, grammar, composition techniques that may have been drummed into your head back in grade school, and all the other reasons for hesitation—poor handwriting, the "correct" paper, not enough time—and just let your thoughts flow. You may be standing at the kitchen counter while dinner is simmering—take the opportunity to share a friend's happiness.

A letter of congratulation is most effective while the news is still fresh in your mind. Don't make the mistake of writing it in your thoughts and

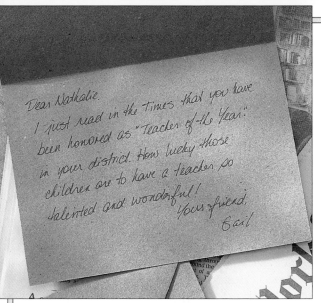

Dear Nathalie,

I just read in the Times that you have been honored as "Teacher of the Year" in your district. How lucky those children are to have a teacher so talented and wonderful!

Your friend,
Gail

phrasing, think instead about being generous and lavish, yet always sincere, with your praise. Such a letter represents a golden opportunity for you to extend your hand to a friend, relative, or associate, to give someone an affectionate hug or a pat on the back. It conveys a generosity of spirit and could easily work to renew or strengthen a special friendship or bond.

storing it there until tomorrow or until you have an opportunity to sit and relax and contemplate the best phrasing. Write it now! It doesn't require research, you don't have to fill up a page, and you don't have to wait for inspiration. The event is the inspiration.

This is a letter so easy to write, in fact, that you may be tempted to complicate it. Instead of concentrating on words and

It may not be necessary to mark the occasion of a birthday, anniversary, promotion, or engagement with a personal card or letter, but think of how even one small sentence can provide someone with an enor-

Dear Eugenia and Tony,

I was thrilled to receive the announcement of your marriage in Summergrove last Wednesday. Jim and I send you both our best wishes for every happiness.

Do let us know when you return to New Jersey so we can congratulate you in person.

Affectionately,

Judy

Steven Lewis Foster

Dear Janis,
We hear that Bobby has graduated with honors from Yale. You must be so proud, and we are very happy for you. Please give Bobby our best wishes for every future success.

Sincerely yours,
Steve

mous lift. It will be a letter that's saved and remembered with deep appreciation for a lifetime.

A congratulatory note on the marriage of people you count among your friends, such as this one from Judy, could include a bit of rice or birdseed.

For a neighbor you see occasionally, or a former colleague, a thoughtful note acknowledges your friendship.

If the occasion to congratulate a relative, friend, neighbor, or coworker arises, view it as an opportunity. It is cause for happiness in a world that too often delivers sadness and bad news. It's a chance for you to enhance someone else's happiness as well as your own.

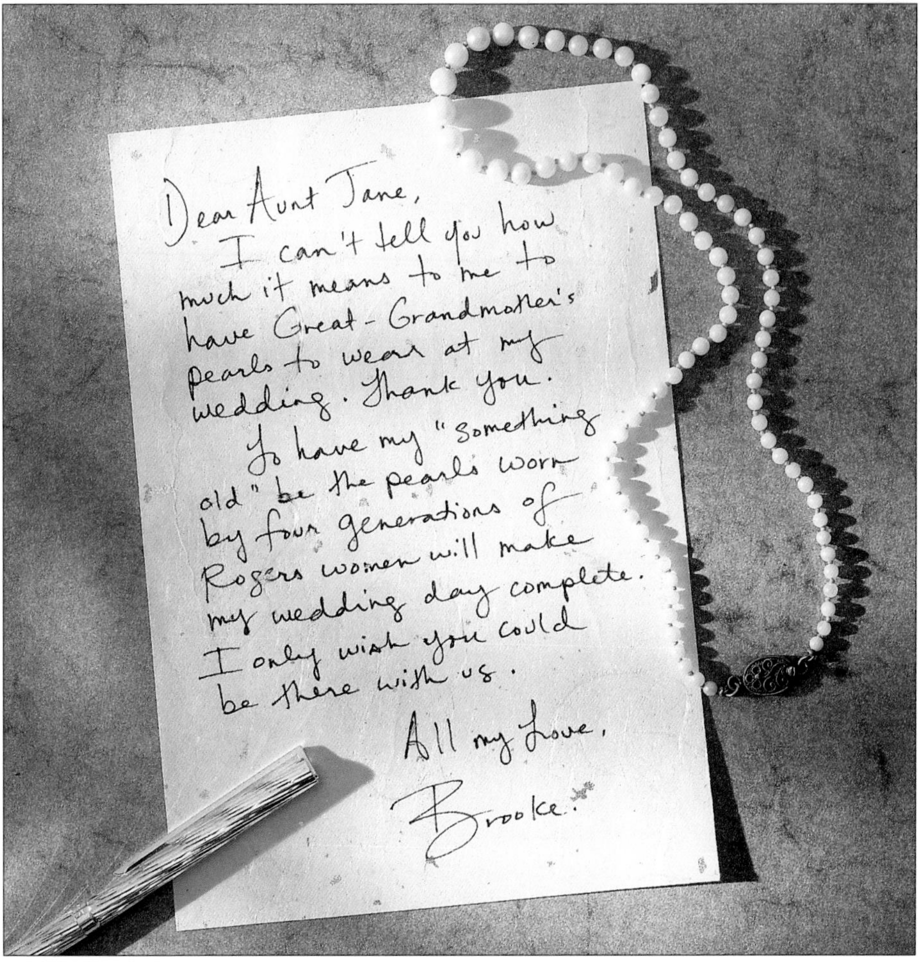
Dear Aunt Jane,
I can't tell you how much it means to me to have Great-Grandmother's pearls to wear at my wedding. Thank you.
To have my "something old" be the pearls worn by four generations of Rogers women will make my wedding day complete. I only wish you could be there with us.
All my Love,
Brooke.

Thank You

Gratitude is the rosemary
of the heart.

—Minna Antrim

A thank-you letter is very likely among the most frequently sent correspondence, surpassed only by birthday cards. Just look at the number of preprinted thank-you notes on the shelves at card shops and stationers. This chapter suggests some ways for you to express your own sentiments of appreciation genuinely and personally. After reading this, you will never again be tempted to buy someone else's thoughts.

Most of us learned to write our "bread and butter" notes when we were small children. Grandmother would send yet another pair of hand-crocheted slippers, and Mother would insist on a gracious thank-you letter as promptly as possible.

*S*INCERE WORDS ARE NOT THAT GRAND.

–

Chinese proverb

Today, more often than not, we use the telephone to express our appreciation for a gift, a dinner party, a flower arrangement, or a thoughtful gesture. In your heart, of course, you know a handwritten note would have more meaning. A letter written in your own hand and addressed to a special individual is personal, intimate, and expressive. It never comes at the wrong time the way a phone call can. Personal correspondence has become a rarity today, so a letter takes on greater importance.

Did someone call just to see how you are? Send a quick note of thanks for her thoughtfulness. She'll be touched and feel rewarded for her efforts.

The next time your husband gives you flowers, pen a note on pretty paper and tuck it into the breast pocket of his suit or in his briefcase. If it is your style, spritz a little of your scent on the paper before you put it in the envelope. Picture his delight when he comes across your little thank-you note!

When you write to say thank you for a visit at a friend's house, try to recap some of the highlights of your stay. Mention the food, the ambience, the hilarious evening of games, the perfect weather, the newly decorated library. Relive on paper the delight you felt in visiting your friends for the evening.

If your children are too young to write their own thank-you notes, write one yourself and include a drawing by your youngster or a photo of the child playing with the toy Nana or Godmother sent.

When a friend remembers your birthday with flowers, save a bloom to dry or press in a book and send it with your thank-you note.

Dear Nana,

Thank you so much for the paint set you sent to Cristina. My refrigerator is already full of her beautiful creations.

Here is one she painted especially for you.

Love,
Julia

Don't overlook the small gestures, such as to your child's teacher for doing something special. Acknowledge them with a simple handwritten thank-you:

We appreciate the extra understanding you have given Timmy during the divorce. It's been hard on him, but you've made it a little easier.

Thank a neighbor for picking up your mail and watering the plants while you were away:

We are so grateful to have such a thoughtful neighbor. Thanks for all your help.

There are many little favors that deserve recognition—your elderly father's neighbor mowing the lawn, your tennis instructor helping you perfect your forehand, or your child making dinner when you didn't feel well:

I am a lucky mother to have such a thoughtful child.

Be careful not to forget the people who go out of their way to help you—the youngster who found your dog when he wandered away or the librarian who searched for information you needed:

Thank you for your prompt and courteous service. You saved me hours of time in my research.

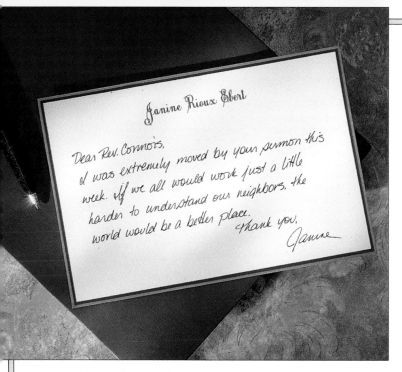

Janine Rioux Ebert

Dear Rev. Connors,

I was extremely moved by your sermon this week. If we all would work just a little harder to understand our neighbors, the world would be a better place.

thank you,

Janine

Each contact with a human being is so rare, so precious, one should preserve it.

—

Anaïs Nin
(1903–1977)

   And remember to acknowledge people who show their kindness by performing their jobs exceptionally well, like the sales clerk at a favorite store who called to let you know a new shipment just arrived or the clergyman whose sermon was especially inspiring.

   It is very easy to pick up the phone and say thank you. But once it is said, the message is gone. A written message that expresses the depth and sincerity of your gratitude for whatever favor or gesture takes on a life of its own and can be treasured by the person who receives it.

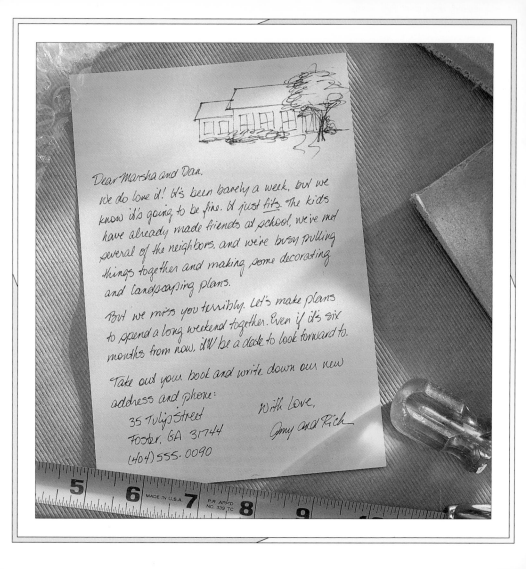

Dear Marsha and Dan,

We do love it! It's been barely a week, but we know it's going to be fine. It just _fits_. The kids have already made friends at school, we've met several of the neighbors, and we're busy pulling things together and making some decorating and landscaping plans.

But we miss you terribly. Let's make plans to spend a long weekend together. Even if it's six months from now, it'll be a date to look forward to.

Take out your book and write down our new address and phone:

35 Tulip Street
Foster, GA 31744
(404) 555-0090

With Love,
Amy and Rich

Announcements

*How much the greatest event it is
that ever happened in the world!
And how much the best!*

—Charles James Fox
1749–1806

While announcements are never obligatory, they are recommended for news of any number of events: engagements, marriages, a new baby, a divorce, a graduation, a change of address, the opening of a professional office, bringing in a new associate, a retirement, the publication of a book, the establishment of a memorial scholarship.

The one obvious detail to keep in mind about news is simple: Once it's a week or two old, it's not news anymore. A birth announcement sent three months later, when the baby has already grown out of "newborn" sizes, lacks fizz. The reaction to an announcement handled in this way is "Oh, the Smiths had a baby around Labor Day," rather than "Good news! The Smiths just had a boy!"

Often, birth announcements are telephoned, but how much more poignant and long lasting a short note on stationery, or even a scribbled message on a preprinted, fill-in card. Certainly, it wouldn't take longer than a telephone call, and in many cases, it would be infinitely easier. (Don't count on having the energy, in full-blown post-partum, to summon the diplomatic skill needed to ease a chatty Aunt Bess off the phone.)

For announcing an engagement, a short letter to those near and dear can

As cold waters to a thirsty soul, so is good news from a far country.

—

Proverbs

make your news ever so special. (According to Emily Post, an engraved announcement of an engagement is not in good taste.) A preprinted, fill-in card with a short personal note from you is fine to announce the family is moving to Georgia, as is an engraved card to formally announce your marriage to a long list of family members, friends, and business associates.

The formal wedding announcement is the same as the wedding invitation itself in nearly everything but the wording. The notepaper, the engraving, two envelopes if desired, the manner of addressing the envelopes all follow the same rules. Emily Post recommends that, unlike the traditional wedding invitation, the announcement include the family of the groom.

Mr. and Mrs. Patrick Wiler Dugen
have the honour of announcing
the marriage of their daughter
Katherine Lynn
to
Mr. Joseph Andrew Williston
on Saturday, the twelfth of August
One thousand nine hundred and eighty-nine
Saint Patrick's Cathedral
New York

Mr. and Mrs. Robert Lopez
have the happiness to announce
the adoption of
Iris Maria
aged 12 months

The brief note above is proper form for a formal announcement of an adoption to friends and relatives.

On a bright yellow paper with your own rendition of your new house drawn in green ink in the corner of the paper (this is especially effective if you're not an architect or an artist), your change-of-address announcement could read something like Amy and Rick's on page 54.

Employ diplomacy and use a "quiet" stationery when announcing a divorce, as Claudette did.

Accountants, doctors, attorneys, and other professionals can send a simple card, personalized with a short message if possible, announcing they have opened a practice. For the professional relocating her practice, an engraved card or a signed letter is appropriate. Even though the letter is addressed to "Dear Clients," professionals would be well advised to take the time, if at all possible, to pen a short, personal message: "We were virtually spilling out into the hallway! Our new, larger space works beautifully."

Announcements keep you up to date and in touch with relatives, friends, associates, and clients. It's good for personal relations and good for business. It can encourage others to share their own news and thereby open the door to new possibilities. Announcements give us all a chance to keep personal and professional relationships connected, fresh, and up-to-date.

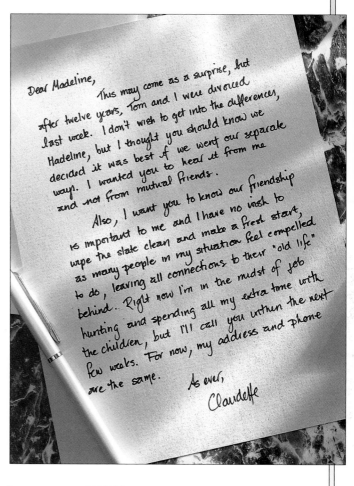

Dear Madeline,

This may come as a surprise, but after twelve years, Tom and I were divorced last week. I don't wish to get into the differences, Madeline, but I thought you should know we decided it was best if we went our separate ways. I wanted you to hear it from me and not from mutual friends.

Also, I want you to know our friendship is important to me and I have no wish to wipe the slate clean and make a fresh start, as many people in my situation feel compelled to do, leaving all connections to their "old life" behind. Right now I'm in the midst of job hunting and spending all my extra time with the children, but I'll call you within the next few weeks. For now, my address and phone are the same.

As ever,
Claudette

9

From

Parent to Child

The child is the root of the heart.

—Carolina Maria de Jesus

Because we live so closely with our children when they are young, we seldom have a real need to communicate with them with the written word. And when they are older, we are much more likely to pick up the phone to share our news and thoughts. There are times, however, when a parent wants a message to be more permanent and enduring. In "From Parent to Child," we take a new look at ways to create lasting mementos of parental love and affection and to express our deep feelings to our children.

Children are a special gift—each one a unique and special being. Our rela-tionships with our children can be lov-ing, stormy, playful, cool, and intense— all in a single day!

Yet the bond of parent-hood is inescapably with us and grows stronger each day as our children inch toward adulthood and indepen-dence. Then our relationships with them take on new mean-ings and nuances. If we are lucky and have been able to sow the seeds of respect and friendship along with love, we will continue to share in the excitements, joys, and sorrows of their lives as they mature and have their own children.

How many parents put down in writ-ing the depth of their love? Not nearly

> GIVE A LITTLE LOVE TO A CHILD AND YOU GET A GREAT DEAL BACK.
>
> —
>
> John Ruskin The Crown of Wild Olive, *1866*

enough! But the opportunities for parent-to-child notes of love, news, encouragement, advice, and humor are endless. Think about all the times you send your child off to school with a book bag and lunch box. How much more special that nutritious lunch would be if it included a little note saying "I hope you are having a good day today," or "Mommy and Daddy are thinking of you."

How reassured your youngster would feel if, midway through her schoolday, she found a card like the one from Mom on page 60.

There are so many times that notes to your children are appropriate. Sometimes, they are not meant to be read until sometime long in the future. For example, write a loving note—or a long series of notes in the form of a diary or journal—to your yet-to-be-born child telling how you feel about the pending birth. Share your feelings of anticipation and wonder. Add little line drawings of your expanding stomach or how you visualize the baby floating inside you.

As you work toward selecting the perfect name for your child, write the choices down with a few lines about why you chose them. You might even try some of them on for size:

Dear little Thomas

or

Dearest Melanie

When you feel the first flutterings of life, jot down the time and place on a blank note card. Record your feelings about that incredible moment when your

child suddenly becomes a physical part of your life for the first time.

Soon after the birth of your new baby, take a moment to write a letter. Welcome the baby to the world and tell how much this birth means to you.

Mark important occasions in your child's life, such as birthdays, big accomplishments, recitals, a bar mitzvah, or a confirmation, with little notes—some to be read now and others to save as a gift.

If you go away for a few days and leave your children behind, hide notes on funny cards in places where they will find them—under a pillow, next to the toothbrushes, taped to the television screen, in pockets of jackets or jeans, even in the refrigerator.

Send a short note to your son or daughter to arrive on the first day of a

*M*OTHER'S LOVE IS EVER IN ITS SPRING.

—

French proverb

new job. It need not say much—just a word of encouragement and praise. "I'm so proud of you."

Letters from home are so important when one is far away. Send notes every week to a young person at boarding school or college. Include clippings from your hometown newspaper and lots of newsy items about friends, family, and goings-on.

Write a letter to your son or daughter on the eve of his or her wedding. Share your thoughts, wishes, and love.

As you are about to become a grandparent, put your feelings in writing and address them to your son or daughter.

Parenthood, from the first tiny cry of life, through all its stages and ups and downs, is forever. How appropriate then to make your written messages of love, of sharing, and of caring last forever, too.

Dearest Samantha,

It's hard for me to realize that you're getting married tomorrow morning. At the risk of sounding silly, I can't help but say it seems like only yesterday that I brought you home from the hospital. It was only a few hours ago that you rode a bike for the first time, and just a minute or so since you earned your degree.

Now that you are about to become a wife — of a wonderful young man, I'd like to add! — there seem to be so many things left undone and unsaid. The one thing that cannot go unsaid is how much I love you. You will always be my firstborn — my beautiful, talented daughter.

And my special wish for you on your wedding day is that you will be as happy in your life with your new husband as Daddy and I have been in ours.

Your loving,
Mom

Extra Special
Notes and Letters

*Happiness is made
to be shared.*

–French proverb

Most of us don't realize the extraordinary power contained in one tiny, thoughtful gesture. Without exaggeration, it can forge a lasting bond and—trite as it sounds—bring the sun into the room on the darkest November day.

The sister-in-law, for instance, who took a candid shot of you and your infant daughter as you arrived home from the hospital has surprised you by sending it to you mounted in a frame she decorated herself. Her three simple words, "All my love," on a plain sheet of paper were worth more than all the expensive toys, the engraved silver bank, and even the smocked pinafore that you got from others. She could have simply addressed a card to your daughter with a store-bought gift, but in choosing this simple, homemade approach, she made a powerful statement about her feelings of affection for you and your child.

Or consider the college friend you went to Italy with during senior year who sent you a picture she took then at the Roman Forum at dusk. On a note she wrote simply, "Remember the legend that we could hear Caesar's army returning to Rome? Why don't we plan another trip with our husbands and try again?" How different the impact of her request would have been if she called one

> $\mathcal{W}$ HERE YOUR
> TREASURE IS,
> THERE WILL
> YOUR HEART
> BE ALSO.
> —
> *Luke, The New
> Testament*

evening as you were just sitting down to balance your checkbook and said, "How do you feel about coming with us to Italy next summer?"

Do some people just know how to do nice things? Or do they take a few extra seconds to think about how? Read through the ideas here and try to cultivate the habit of developing your own thoughtful gestures. Keep a notepad handy to jot down ideas as you think of them.

Send a small scented sachet envelope with a short note to someone you know could use a day brightener.

Send your child's preschool artwork to Grandma with a short note from the child written on the back.

Look for special note cards made of parchment or other interesting papers that are hand-painted and decorated with lace and ribbon. Some are even suitable for framing. Or try making your own. Buy some nice paper, some construction or foil paper, search around for some lace and a few bits of fabric and yarn, and make your own Valentine's Day card, for example. Perhaps just the *impression of your lips on a white card would make a fine greeting. (Why buy a Valentine's Day card that features someone else's lips?)*

Send a string of tiny jingle bells attached to a Christmas card to a niece, a nephew, or to a friend's child.

Send your new neighbors a note of welcome along with the names of the best restaurants in your area. (Be sure to take the children into consideration.)

To a daughter who is spending her first Christmas away from home, send the recipe for cookies you always made together.

In the dead of winter, assemble a bunch of "warm weather" pictures — beaches, palm trees, burning sun, sunglasses, san-

dals, people swimming in pools — and send them to a friend who's snowbound. Ask her if she'd like to plan a summer vacation with your family.

Send self-addressed, stamped envelopes and writing paper to a child who is away from home.

As a dear neighbor drives down the street for the last time on her way to her new home in another state, hand her an envelope of seeds taken from your garden with a short reminder taped on the back to write the first chance she gets.

Pen a special proverb or a loving message you know will be appreciated by an old friend. (For ideas, look through any of the many books of quotations.)

Send a cassette tape of a song that befits the mood of a friend or coworker. This can be very serious or entirely tongue-in-cheek.

Pop a Hershey's Kiss into the envelope before sealing a love letter.

A SMALL GIFT
IS BETTER
THAN A GREAT
PROMISE
—
*German
proverb*

Be creative when sending a gift in the mail. Instead of simply enclosing a card with your name on it, take an extra minute to personalize your message, to mark it with your personality. Here are some thoughts:

If you're sending a gift of airline tickets, make a paper airplane and attach the tickets to the wings. If you don't have the tickets yet, or if they are to be picked up at the airport, make your own. Another idea would be to attach the tickets to something that speaks of the destination—a cowboy hat for Dallas, for instance, a plastic Eiffel Tower if it's Paris, or a pair of Mickey Mouse ears if it's Orlando.

When sending a silver bowl for a wedding gift, your note could say, "Best wishes to both of you. Our hope is that this will be the centerpiece on your dining room table at your twenty-fifth anniversary celebration."

*S*HE SAT DOWN AND READ THE LETTER OVER AGAIN; BUT THERE WERE PHRASES THAT INSISTED ON BEING READ MANY TIMES, THEY HAD A LIFE OF THEIR OWN SEPARATE FROM THE OTHERS...

Katherine Anne Porter,
Flowering Judas and Other Stories

Send theater tickets along with glowing reviews of the show.

Send a picture frame for a christening with the words, "Savor each moment. It goes by so quickly."

There are so many ways to be creative and to say what you mean. The old adage that actions speak louder than words applies here. Stretch your imagination a little and see how much fun you can have with this. It may inspire your friends to do the same.

Index